The Body and the Blood

A Biblical Study of Christ and Communion

An Invitation to an Active, Vibrant, Intimate Celebration with the Savior, Jesus Christ!

Randy J. Widrick

DEDICATION

*To Josephine (Joey), my hero, friend, and wife
of 38 years who saw me not for who I was,
but for whom Christ could make me.*

TABLE OF CONTENTS

CONTRIBUTORS

Proverbs 15:22 states, "With many counselors they [plans] succeed." A special "thank you" to the contributors to this study and the wisdom and insight they provided.

Henry Ausby
Senior Pastor
Hands of Hope Ministries
Free Methodist Church
Binghamton, NY

John Adam Widrick
Youth Pastor
Calvary's Love Church
Johnson City, NY

Josephine A. Widrick
Lifestyle Coach

Valerie Hoffman
Editor

INTRODUCTION

"Everyone who is of the truth hears My voice." Jesus Christ made this dramatic declaration as He stood before Pilate facing death by crucifixion. Pilate responded with a statement that echoes down to us more than 2000 years later, **"What is truth?"** This is a question you will have to answer for yourself. Your answer will determine your actions. Your answer will determine your destiny in this life and in the next. Is there even a next life? Is there absolute truth? If there is absolute truth, who has it? Leaders? Politicians? Professors? Doctors? Scientists? Priests? Ministers? Our parents? Me? You?

Have you ever taken the time to question what you believe to be true? Can you clearly state where you find truth? Is mine different from yours? The modern argument when opposing viewpoints are discussed is the easy-out statement, "Well, that's what you believe, and I respect that, but I don't see it that way!" You are welcome to believe whatever you choose to believe. We respect and protect that God-given freedom.

Many years ago, I sought desperately to find the truth, the meaning in life, something I could live for…something I believed in so strongly that I would die for it. Have you found something like that? I didn't find it in my career. I was a master at messing up relationships, both mine and others. The answer for me wasn't in education, making money, or driving fast cars. My experience with drugs was short-lived, thank God, after the first "trip" was a bad one. Except for the prayers of my faithful mom, the situations I found myself in could easily have resulted in an early death. Finding no answers and feeling life had no meaning, thoughts and plans for suicide formulated in my mind. If there is no truth, no purpose, no meaning, then what is the reason for living? I had tried everything…almost everything. I looked on the shelf of my efficiency apartment. My eye landed on my old, dusty Bible. I remembered all that I had been taught when I was a child. The words and verses from my past blazed out at me. That night, I met TRUTH. He had a name…**Jesus Christ**! I remembered His words in John 14:6, "I am the way, and the truth and the life. No one comes to the Father but through Me."

The Bible said that if I believed in Him and invited Him to take over my life, He would forgive me of my sin, come into my heart, and live in me. I believed what He said. Thoughts of hopelessness, despair, and suicide were driven out by a candle light of life and love that has been burning brighter and brighter for more than 40 years.

Over the years, each and every one of His promises that I have trusted has proven to be true, as He said. I have found the Bible to be the absolute Word of God. My desire is to look only at what the Bible says about Communion, not to add to the Scripture with my own opinion, and then to show you what Christ did because of His love for you. You, as a reader, will have one of three common responses to what you read in these pages about the Bible, Jesus Christ, and Communion.

1. You will choose to believe the Word of God and act on it by faith receiving and appropriating all of His benefits for you.

2. You will think about it and want to examine it further.

3. You will reject it as foolishness and may not even finish the study.

Even the men and women who lived when Christ walked this earth had the exact same responses. Mankind has not changed very much; we just think we have. My task here is not to argue with you; it is to proclaim what the Bible says about

Communion, about Christ. My prayer is that with an open mind you will consider the truth contained here, so you can experience all of the spiritual blessings provided for you in Christ Jesus.

The Bible, in its original languages, is the true, inerrant Word of God in all that it addresses, including history and the cosmos. Statements of faith from two major denominations are included for you to review. May you be blessed as you study and learn what the Bible says about the Person of Jesus Christ as celebrated in the Communion service, and may you experience all of the blessings that are yours in His Body and His Blood.

Statements of Biblical Inerrancy

The Bible is God's written Word, uniquely inspired by the Holy Spirit. It bears unerring witness to Jesus Christ, the living Word. As attested by the early church and subsequent councils, it is the trustworthy record of God's revelation, completely truthful in all it affirms. It has been faithfully preserved and proves itself true in human experience.

The Scriptures have come to us through human authors who wrote, as God moved them, in the languages and literary forms of their times. God continues, by the illumination of the Holy Spirit, to speak through this Word to each generation and culture. The Bible has authority over all human life. It teaches the truth about God, His creation, His people and only Son and the destiny of humankind. It also teaches the way of salvation and the life of faith. Whatever is not found in the Bible nor can be proved by it is not required as an article of belief or as necessary to salvation.

The Authority of the Scriptures #108
Free Methodist Book of Discipline, 2015

THE SCRIPTURES INSPIRED

The Scriptures, both the Old and New Testaments, are verbally inspired of God and are the revelation of God to man, the infallible, authoritative rule of faith and conduct.

- *2 Timothy 3:15-17*

- *1 Thessalonians 2:13*

- *2 Peter 1:21*

The Assemblies of God Fundamental Truths
www.ag.org

WHAT IS COMMUNION?

Also referred to as the Lord's Supper and the Eucharist, Communion is a very important ordinance of the Christian church, believed by some groups to be a sacrament. Its tremendous significance is that it was instituted directly and personally by the Lord Jesus Christ on the night he was betrayed. Two elements are served in each Communion service, the bread and the wine (the cup), symbolizing the body and the blood of our Savior and His wonderful, substitutionary sacrifice for our sin and the sins of all humanity. In its true Scriptural teaching, it should be an active, vibrant, and intimate celebration with other believers and most of all, with the Savior Himself, experiencing His presence and rejoicing in the blessings of the precious sacrifice of His body and His blood in all aspects of our lives. As I said…it SHOULD be…but most of the time, it isn't.

Sadly, having been involved in different churches and denominations for the past 50 years of my life, I have experienced varying practices, teachings, and questions concerning Communion. Questions arise as to its significance and its meaning: What do the elements represent? How often should we take it? Who should be allowed; who should NOT be allowed? Should we forbid anyone? Should we allow children to take Communion? What does the bread mean? What does the wine (cup) mean? Can we take Communion at home, or does it have to be administered by a minister or priest, and on and on.

What does the Bible say? This brief study is a look at what the Scripture says and a call to the return and practice of the Communion service to a pure form, unchained from added unnecessary and often non-Scriptural traditions, rituals, and practices put in place by church leaders. The true Communion service is a remembrance and celebration of Jesus Christ and who He is. In most cases that I have witnessed, Communion has become little more than a traditional ritual, just something we do off and on, maybe weekly, maybe less often…taken briefly at the end of a service, lasting maybe ten minutes. Those who participate usually do not know or have not been correctly taught the tremendous significance of both the bread and the cup, how they are a representation of the sacrifice of His body and His blood. Regretfully, I am not totally convinced that those who administer Communion are even aware of the blessings promised and the conditions required in order for individuals to correctly make the decision to take (or not to take) Communion. If the leaders are aware, it is not clearly evident in the instruction given.

Let's do a quick assessment.

- ✓ In your Communion service has there been solid teaching about the significance of both the body and the blood of Christ?

- ✓ Did you know there are wonderful blessings from "judging (discerning) the body" correctly?

- ✓ Are you aware of the connection to the Passover Feast?

- ✓ Prior to taking Communion, have you been instructed to "examine yourself" spiritually?

- ✓ Are you aware that there are warnings of taking Communion in what the Apostle Paul calls an "unworthy manner"? Do you know what they are?

✓ Did you know that it possibly may be more of a blessing for you NOT to take Communion?

The author of New Testament Communion practice is the Lord Jesus Himself, which He taught to His disciples on the night He was betrayed. The Communion service has deep roots in the Old Testament, which we will examine. Our answers and our understanding will come only from the Holy Spirit inspired teachings of the Bible, both the Old and the New Testament.

Do NOT Add, Take Away or Modify

Modern society, and sadly, many church leaders and ministers believe that they have the right to add to the Scriptures, take away from the Scriptures, and modify or omit certain Scriptures that are difficult. Their belief, and maybe yours, is that the Bible, in its original languages, is not the inspired, inerrant Word of God. What does the Bible say about itself:

> "All Scripture is inspired by God and profitable for teaching,
> for reproof, for correction, for training in righteousness;
> so that the man [and woman] of God may be adequate,
> equipped for every good work."
>
> II Timothy 3:16-17

"Forever, O Lord, Your word is settled in heaven."

Psalm 119:89

Jesus Himself said in Luke 21:33, "Heaven and earth will pass away, but My words will not pass away." The Bible is the absolute truth of God and should be our sole authority in all of the areas it addresses. The Word of God is very clear that we are NOT to take the position of omitting, altering, adding, or taking away from the Scripture:

"Let not many of you become teachers, my
brethren, knowing that such as we will
incur a stricter judgment."

James 3:1

"Be diligent to present yourself approved to God as a workman who does not need to be ashamed, accurately handling the word of truth."

2 Timothy 2:15

If anyone adds to them, God will add to him the plagues which are written in this book; and if anyone takes away from the words of the book of this prophecy, God will take away his part from the tree of life and from the holy city...

Revelation 22:18-19

Although the last verses are commands from the Book of Revelation, we are given a strong, cautionary warning that we are to be <u>exact</u> in handling God's Word. The prophet Jeremiah in delivering a judgment prophecy was strictly told by God, "Do not omit a word", (see Jeremiah 26:2). We are to be painstakingly diligent as teachers to correctly divide the Word of God. We are not to add, take way, modify or omit portions we do not like. Therefore, in this study we will be especially watchful so as not to extend beyond what the Scripture plainly states, neither will we include human or church tradition in the study unless it agrees with and comes under the authority of the Scripture.

A True Story

Mary Ann, a friend, struggled with the meaning and purpose of the Communion service, not really understanding it but being encouraged to participate whenever she attended a service. She participated along with everyone else. Knowing many people in the community, she observed several acquaintances who lived horrible and not-nice lives during the week, but on Sunday or another weekly service, they freely took Communion. During the following weeks she continued to observe the same nasty behavior, but the same people were taking Communion over and over again. Her confusion was this, *"Can people live any way they choose, do whatever they want, and then take Communion every week, and God forgives it all and gives them a clean slate? Just because they attend a church? Is it just a ritual? What is the meaning? What is the purpose if the behavior never changes?"*

You may have some of the same questions. When Communion is administered publicly in a church setting, usually the passage in 1 Corinthians 11 is read, with minimal or no instruction. Who takes Communion? In most cases, whoever wants---men, women, children, everybody! Again, there are no conditions, no guidelines. Scripturally, it may be a blessing for some, but it also may be a negative for others because they do not know or have not been taught what the Bible says.

Different denominations and even churches within a denomination may have varying practices, most of which may be fine as long as they are subject to the teachings of Scripture. We are going to examine what the Bible states about Communion, so you can correctly decide. The Apostle Paul and Silas traveled to Berea and began to teach in the synagogue. Even after hearing the Gospel directly from the mouth of Paul, the church of Berea checked the accuracy of his teaching against the Scriptures:

> "...they [the church at Berea] received the word with great eagerness, examining the Scriptures daily to see whether these things were so."
>
> Acts 17:11

Don't believe what I write here on face value...<u>check it out for yourself to see if it is true</u>! All of the relevant passages, quoted from the *New American Standard Bible*, will be printed for your reference. Prayerfully study each of them, seeking the truth. In certain key passages, I will refer to the words in the original languages to make sure I am giving the passage the correct meaning. This will provide you with the information you need to draw your own conclusions. Communion, was instituted by our Lord Jesus Christ personally. In I Corinthians 11:23, the Apostle Paul, regarding Communion, states, "For I received from the Lord that which I delivered to you." Because our Lord instituted it and **directly** gave specific instruction to the Apostle Paul, isn't it a wise choice to go to the Lord as the source in order to determine its proper meaning, practice, and conditions?

Wouldn't the blessings, commands, and conditions of the author, Jesus, supersede what any church, denomination, or person might say, regardless of how important you believe they are? Think with me for a moment. Who would have more of an authoritative answer other than the creator and author, regardless of the topic?

The Communion celebration has <u>three</u> focal points concerning the Lord Jesus Christ and His ministry to us. By participating in Communion:

1. We look to the past in loving remembrance of the life of Jesus Christ, His death, burial, resurrection, and ascension.

2. We celebrate His current presence in us and with us.

3. We publicly proclaim the fact that we are His disciples and He is coming again for us.

It is a phenomenally active and powerful celebration of fellowship and intimacy with our Lord. Ask the Holy Spirit, our blessed Teacher, to illumine the Word and reveal the truth to you. May God bless you richly as you study, meditate, and participate "as often as you like" in the celebration that is His Body and His Blood.

IN REMEMBRANCE OF ME

Communion is detailed in three of the four Gospels (Matthew 26:20-30; Mark 14:17-26; Luke 22:7-23) and then in the first letter to the Corinthian church, Chapter 11:23-32, quoted here, which is the passage that will be our main focus:

> For I received from the Lord that which I also delivered to you, that the Lord Jesus in the night which He was betrayed took bread; and when He had given thanks, He broke it and said, "This is My body, which is for you; do this in remembrance of Me." In the same way, He took the cup also after supper, saying, "This cup is the new covenant in My blood; do this, as often as you drink it, in remembrance of Me." For as often as you eat this bread and drink the cup, you proclaim the Lord's death till He comes. Therefore whoever eats the bread or drinks the cup of the Lord in an unworthy manner, shall be guilty of the body and the blood of the Lord. But a man must examine himself, and in so doing he is to eat of the bread and drink of the cup. For he who eats and drinks, eats and drinks judgment to himself if he does not judge the body rightly. For this reason many among you are weak and sick, and a number sleep. But if we judged ourselves rightly, we would not be judged. But when we are

judged, we are disciplined by the Lord so that we will not be condemned along with the world.

In Communion, our celebration is in remembrance of the past, the present, and the future of our Lord Jesus Christ, who took on human flesh and walked among us. Have you taken the time to ask, "Why"?

Why did Jesus Christ, the second Person of the Trinity, choose to become flesh? What was the reason? Was it part of a divine plan? Was it necessary for Christ to leave the glory and splendor of heaven, become a baby, and ultimately be crucified on a cross? Before we can understand the divine purpose of the human life and work of Jesus Christ, we have to come to grips with our situation, our true condition before a holy God. What was the problem with humanity that necessitated God to take on human form? We have to ask the difficult human question which we easily avoid, "What did I do to cause this?" Let's take a step back in time and peek into a beautiful garden of harmony and peace, a picture of what the earth was like before it changed (See Genesis 1, 2).

The Garden of Eden

Often people ask me, "Where did all this evil in the world come from?" The answer is simple, "It wasn't always this way. It wasn't this way in the beginning." The Garden of Eden was a perfect place. The Bible says that God saw all of His creation and pronounced that it was "very good". All of creation was in harmony. Man and woman walked and talked with God in the cool of the evening. Sickness, disease, division, strife and murder were not present in this beautiful place. In Genesis 2: 16, 17, God gave Adam one command only to obey:

> The Lord God commanded the man, saying, "From any tree of the garden you may eat freely; but from the tree of the knowledge of good and evil you may not eat, for in the day that you eat from it, you shall surely die."

One command only! Think about it! If the beautiful garden had no possible exit, no free will, no ability for man to choose, then man is nothing more than a prisoner in a gorgeous prison. Even to this day, God desires our worship and service, not out of force or compulsion, but because we love Him. The Garden of Eden had to have an opportunity for man to exercise his free moral choice. Eve, tempted by the serpent, ate from the forbidden tree and gave some to her husband, who was with her

(See Genesis 2, 3). Immediately, both the man and woman became spiritually dead, even though they were alive physically. By the sin of Adam and Eve, the authority over the earth that was given to man and woman by God, was transferred to Satan. The purity and perfection of the Garden of Eden was disrupted. Sin had entered. The majesty of man and woman walking with God, communicating with God in the garden, was gone.

Man was separated from God, separated from himself, and separated from his wife; even nature was placed under a curse. Sin, sickness, disease, and death, previously unknown before, had now contaminated the world. Murder soon entered the human race when Cain killed Abel. Soon after, the Bible gives an account of the war of the kings. Man and woman were spiritually lost and fallen, separated by sin from their purpose and their Creator. That same sinful nature has been passed down from generation to generation, even to you and me, infecting the entire human race. We love to blame God for the problems in the world, but they are the result of man's rebellion against a holy God. A great chasm that man cannot cross by his own good works separates the entire human race from fellowship with a holy God. Every religion tries, to no avail, to bridge the gap, to tell us that we can work our way back to God, somehow by our own good deeds. It is impossible through human effort.

But I'm a Good Person

I hear this all the time and actually, I agree. I know many, many people who do good, both in word and deed. I know several who are compassionate and caring, giving to others, even protecting and caring for animals and nature. Many live incredibly moral lives (these are the hardest to convince of the truth). But by what standard are you grading yourself? Are you totally perfect? Without fault? Never made a mistake? I am not. The benefit I had was that I knew I was a bad person, so it was not hard for me to believe what the Bible said. It is God, the Creator, who determines the rules for His creation. We have very little concept of the pure, absolute holiness of God:

> "The fear of the Lord is the <u>beginning</u> of wisdom,
> and knowledge of the Holy One is understanding."
>
> Proverbs 9: 10

His standard for our fellowship and acceptance into His presence is perfection…100% holiness and perfection. Sin and imperfection cannot enter or survive in the presence of a holy God. A friend of mine, Tim, gave $20 to a homeless person one morning. Being quite proud of his generosity he said the following: *"Well, I think I am over the 50% mark, tipping the scales the right way. That should get me into heaven!"* Another friend proudly rated himself as a very good person, better than most, and gave himself a seven out of 10, definitely passing in God's eyes. Somehow, we have adopted and promoted this strange and false teaching that an acceptable score is 50.1%. Whew! Just made it! Not so!! Not even close:

"For all have sinned and fall short of the glory of God."

Romans 3:23

If we say we that we have no sin, we are deceiving ourselves and the truth is not in us. If we confess our sins, He is faithful and just to forgive us our sins and to cleanse us from all unrighteousness. If we say that we have not sinned, we make Him a liar and His word is not in us.

1 John 1: 8-10

We can declare ourselves to be good throughout our entire life. We can compare ourselves to the person next door and justify that we are much better. Every day we can hear the news and see the horrible actions of criminals and then pride ourselves on our own goodness. However, when we stand before a perfectly, pure, holy God and give an account of "every word we have spoken, every deed we have done", we will find that we will fall far short of the glory of God. His only standard is absolute PERFECTION and HOLINESS:

> "For whoever keeps the whole law and yet
> stumbles in <u>one point</u>, he has become guilty of <u>**all**</u>."
>
> James 2:10

God is holy! Can any person ever measure up to a perfect standard in every word and every deed throughout his or her whole life? No lies? Never stole or gossiped? Not one bad thought or coveting what someone else has? No road rage? Never lost your temper? Never took something from your employer because you felt you deserved it? Never spoke harshly to your parents or children? Even Mary Poppins was only "practically perfect" but not completely. Can you measure up? I cannot come even close.

If you believe that at the deepest core of your being you are basically good, then one day you will have the opportunity to convince the eternal God, the Creator of the universe of your perfection. I am not trying to put you down or condemn you. My goal is to attempt to clearly communicate and help you understand what God says about our true spiritual condition so we can receive His cure, be restored, and healed. I can tell the doctor on every visit how well and healthy I am, but when I receive the diagnosis and the remedy is prescribed, am I really going to tell him that he is a liar? I will issue the final test…if you really believe you measure up to a perfect standard, ask someone who knows you well, who loves you enough to be brutally honest, and you will be brought quickly back to reality. Sinful man and woman cannot have fellowship with a pure, holy, righteous God. We are a lost and fallen race. Friends, this is not hard to believe. All we have to do is watch the news, read the history of humanity --- the Holocaust, wars, famines, diseases, cheating, scandals. Even a daily look at social media will show our true condition. We can blame someone else, but God says the sin problem, the sinful nature is in you and me.

God says He is the Eternal Creator. He says mankind has fallen and the human race is infected with a sinful nature separating us from Him. Everyone. You! Me! He says that if we do not believe this, we are calling Him a liar and the truth is not in us. But, we have the free will to believe whatever we choose.

What say You?

Believing the Lie

False teachers also have spread the terrible lie that we have no purpose, that we are simply a product of time, matter, and chance, and that once our life is over we will pass into nothingness. God challenges this destructive lie in Psalm 139: 13-17 as King David proclaims:

> You formed my inward parts; You wove me in my mother's womb. I will give thanks to You, for I am fearfully and wonderfully made; wonderful are Your works, and my soul knows it very well. My frame was not hidden from You, when I was made in secret, and skillfully wrought in the depths of the earth; Your eyes have seen my unformed substance; and in Your book were all written, the days that were ordained for me, when as yet there was not one of them. How precious also are Your thoughts to me, O God!

Does this sound like you are a product of time, matter, and chance? Exactly the opposite! You are a masterpiece of His creative design, the highest achievement of His creation.

Foolish people say that you are a little higher than the animals having evolved from them. Their words bring you down. God says in Psalm 8 that you were made "a little lower than the angels". You were wonderfully designed by Him with a purpose and a plan. You are an eternal being, and you will give an account of your life, every word and deed. Jesus said in Matthew 12:36:

"I tell you that every careless word that people speak,
they shall give an accounting for it in the day of judgment.
For by your words you will be justified, and
by your words you will be condemned."

To understand the love of God for humanity and the necessity of the work of Christ, we must come to grips with our true, fallen condition before a perfect and holy God; only then we can understand and receive His solution for our condition.

The Divine Solution

God could have easily given up on the entire human race and left us in our separated, sinful, imperfect state forever separated and lost. But the Triune God, Father, Son, and Holy Spirit, because of their great love for the human race, already had a plan in place for the redemption and salvation of man.

God loves humanity, desiring passionately to restore man to fellowship with Him, to repair what had been lost in the Garden of Eden, but sin has a penalty. The legal price for sin had to be paid to allow man to have fellowship with a perfectly holy God. Because of His great love for us, He sent Jesus Christ His beloved Son, as a willing sacrifice to pay the penalty for our sin. Thus, He became our Substitute. God, in the person of Jesus Christ, became flesh and dwelt among us. Jesus came into the world to save sinners, to restore us back to a right relationship with God:

"For the wages of sin is death, but the free gift of God is eternal life in Christ Jesus, our Lord."

Romans 6:23

He came to save all men and women. Yes, it was a legal transaction; the penalty for your sin and mine had to be paid by His blood. But far more than that, His was a love affair with humanity, a desire for a loving, restored relationship with you. He came to save you, and He came to deliver you. Communion is a celebration of the historical fact that God, in the Person of Jesus Christ, came to this earth to save us from our sins.

Often, we wrongly believe the false picture of a judgmental Father God holding a sledge hammer over us just waiting for us to mess up…another lie that is perpetuated. Nothing could be further from the truth:

For God so LOVED the world, that He gave His only begotten Son, that whoever believes in Him shall not perish but have eternal life. For God <u>DID NOT</u> send the Son into the world to condemn the world but that the world through Him might be saved.

John 3: 16,17

The Bible, both the Old and New Testaments, is a story of the love of God for a fallen race. Jesus became a willing, necessary sacrifice for all who believe in Him to be completely forgiven of their sins and to be restored to their relationship with God, a relationship of love, joy, and peace.

His Purpose

Jesus Christ, totally God and totally man, came to die for our sins, and to bring us back into fellowship with God. Our sin was imputed to Him. His righteousness was imputed to us. Through Him and only Him can we have access to God:

"I am the way, and the truth and the life; <u>**no one**</u> <u>comes to the Father but through Me."</u>

John 14:6

"There is **<u>one God and one mediator</u>** also between
God and men, the man Christ Jesus, who gave
Himself as a ransom for all…"

1 Timothy 2: 5, 6

Since the Fall of man in the Garden of Eden, the human race has continually invented and promoted many different dead-end paths to God. All of the religions of the world, except Biblical Christianity, through varying methods of self-effort, say that we can work our way back to God through our own good deeds.

It's God's Universe

God makes the rules for His universe, not man or woman, not you and not me. God is holy, and those who approach Him must be holy. We are in desperate need of a Savior. If we can make it to God on our own, by our own goodness, there is absolutely no reason for Christ to come to this earth, be beaten, scourged, and die the horrible death of crucifixion. Jesus Christ came into the world to save sinners, you and me.

His Was A Wonderful Life

We speak often of a person being normal or abnormal. Do you want to know what a normal person should be and act like? Jesus Christ is the perfect example of all that a human is intended to be. With an open and a teachable heart, take the time to examine the life of Jesus closely. Lay aside the things you have heard and believed. Take a closer look at Jesus Himself! Read how He acts, how He feels, how He cares, loves, and communicates. A good place to start is the Gospel of John. John wrote his Gospel for one specific reason:

"...so that you may believe that Jesus is the Christ and that believing, you may have life in His Name."

John 20:31

If you have a desire to know what God is like, look at Jesus. He said, "He who has seen Me, has seen the Father" (John 14:9). Do not make your determination of Christianity based on churches or even on Christians you know as you often may be very disappointed. Look at the life of the Savior Himself. He did not say He was just a prophet, or a good man; His continual claim was that He was God. He healed all who were sick, whether emotionally, mentally, spiritually, or physically. Which person do you find in any of the Gospels (Matthew, Mark, Luke, and John) who came for any form of healing and was turned away? I have read every passage in the four Gospels and researched every time Christ healed someone. He never turned anyone away. He healed them in many different ways, some immediately and others gradually. He had compassion on all who were hurting. He looked on the downtrodden of this world and loved them. He journeyed toward Jerusalem, knowing full well He was to be arrested, beaten, scourged, and then crucified. He knew and willingly embraced His purpose and mission as a substitutionary sacrifice for the sins of the entire human race, including yours and mine. Why? One reason! **<u>LOVE for you and me</u>.** He told His disciples that He would rise from the dead on the third day, and He did, and He appeared physically to more than 500 people <u>after</u> His resurrection. More than 400 prophecies in the Bible were fulfilled in Jesus Christ. He is the Savior. He is my Savior and the Savior to all who will receive Him and believe on His Name. Is that you?

If you have more questions and desire a deeper understanding of the life of Christ, I highly recommend *The Case for Christ*, by Lee Strobel. He was a skeptical journalist who investigated the claims of Christ by interviewing scholars all over the United States. He was moved by the transformation he saw in his wife as a result of her becoming a follower of Christ. The result? In his own words, Strobel, (1998, p.14) states:

> I launched an all-out investigation into the facts surrounding the case for Christianity. Setting aside my self-interest and prejudices as best as I could, I read books, interviewed experts, asked questions, analyzed history, explored archaeology, studied ancient literature, and for the first time in my life picked apart the Bible verse by verse. I plunged into the case with more vigor than with any story I had ever pursued. I applied the training I had received at Yale Law School as well as my experience as legal affairs editor of the *Chicago Tribune*. And over time the evidence of the world—of history, of science, of philosophy, of psychology—began to point toward the unthinkable.

After intense study and research, he also became a passionate, disciple of Christ. As you daily interact with humanity, looking at this crazy world around us, don't you long for the ideals of beauty, perfection, complete honesty, integrity, holiness, loyalty, righteousness, goodness, patience, peace, and most of all, love? I have found all of these characteristics in the most perfect form in Him. All of the ideals that you desire and long for in humanity are manifested in Jesus Christ. Look and see. In Communion, we remember and celebrate in praise and worship His wonderful life.

His Death, Burial, Resurrection

As the second Person of the Trinity, Jesus was completely submitted to God's redemptive plan for the salvation of the human race. Mankind had fallen. He, as the second Adam came to repair what the first Adam had forfeited. He was the willing Substitute to pay the penalty for our sin, to make the way for peace with God. Through faith in Him, we are forgiven of our sins, receive redemption, and have eternal life. As the old hymn states:

"I am redeemed but not with silver,
I am bought but not with gold,
bought with a price, the blood of Jesus,
precious price of love untold."

In Luke 22:41-44, we look at the account of His agony in the Garden of Gethsemane, just prior to His arrest and trial, when He prayed:

"Father, if You are willing, remove this cup from Me; yet not My will, but Yours be done." Now an angel from heaven appeared to Him, strengthening Him. And being in agony He was praying very fervently; and His sweat became like drops of blood, falling down upon the ground.

Why was He in agony? What was the request He was making? The opinion of most commentators, as well as my own paraphrase is: Father, if there is <u>ANY</u> other way to redeem humanity and restore them to you, other than the scourging, the beating and the crucifixion, taking on the sin of the whole world, please remove this cup from Me. If not, Father, then not My will, but Thy will be done.

He lay down His life of His own free will, for us. He was arrested, beaten, scourged and crucified. He was then buried in a garden tomb and rose from the dead, just as He said. Our sin was imputed to Him. By faith in Him, the righteousness of Christ is imputed to us:

> "He [God] made Him [Christ] who knew no sin to be sin on our behalf, so that we might become the righteousness of God in Him [Christ]."
>
> II Corinthians 5:21

He willingly became our Substitute. By faith in Him, our sins are cast "as far as the east is from the west" (see Psalm 103:12), and they are remembered no more. When the redemptive work of Christ was finished, He gave up His life and breathed His last:

"No one has taken it away from Me, but I lay it down on My own initiative. I have authority to lay it down, and I have authority to take it up again."

John 10: 18

Through faith in Christ, we now have peace with God. We have been reconciled back to God through the death of Christ. The price and penalty for our sin has been paid in full. If you have received God's wonderful gift of Christ and trusted Him, your weight of sin has been lifted, forgiven…GONE! God sees you through the righteousness of Jesus Christ. You are accepted! In Christ, God is not angry with you. He has nothing against you. Your slate is clean, completely clean. Forgiven!

"Therefore there is now no condemnation for those who are in Christ Jesus."

Romans 8:1

Randy J. Widrick

The GREAT News of the Gospel

No matter how hard we try, how many good things we do, we come far short of the perfection necessary to enter God's presence. But the wonderful news is that Jesus Christ did it **FOR** us! As an act of pure love, He came and lived a perfect life, completely obedient to the Law. He was beaten, scourged, crucified, bled and died for our sins. He rose again on the third day. He paid the price so that you and I do not have to. What does He ask us to do? Only believe in His finished work for you:

> ...if you confess with your mouth Jesus as Lord [Master] and believe in your heart that God raised Him from the dead, you will be saved; for with the heart a person believes, resulting in righteousness, and with mouth he confesses, resulting in salvation.
>
> Romans 10: 9-10

The chasm and separation between God and man has been bridged by Jesus Christ. We can now have peace with God through faith in Christ.

When we take Communion, we pause and meditate on Him and what He did for us by taking on flesh and being obedient unto death, even death on a cross...for us, that we might be brought back into relationship with God. What a glorious reason to celebrate!

His Ascension

Shortly after He had risen from the dead, He ascended into heaven. Why? So the Holy Spirit of God could come and dwell with us and in us.   When we receive Christ as our Savior, look what the Holy Spirit does, as stated in Ephesians 1: 13-14:

> In Him, you also, after listening to the message of truth, the gospel of your salvation---having also believed, you were sealed in Him with the Holy Spirit of promise, who is given as a pledge of our inheritance, with a view to the redemption of God's own possession, to the praise of His glory.

The Holy Spirit is given to dwell in us as a pledge, a promise, a down payment assuring us that we belong to Christ; He will faithfully complete the work He began in us. We have an inheritance in Him. He will never, ever leave us or forsake us, and then, one day soon, He will come for us. You can be CONFIDENT that this is true. In Christ Jesus, you are born again.

"Therefore if anyone is in Christ, he is a new creature; the old things passed away; behold new things have come."

2 Corinthians 5:17

"For I [Apostle Paul] am CONFIDENT of this very thing, that He who began a good work in you will perfect it until the day of Christ Jesus."

Philippians 1:6

Jesus said, "I came that they might have life, and that they might have it abundantly."

John 10:10

Every purpose and plan of God was good for the human race, to redeem us and bring us back into fellowship with Him through the shed blood of Christ. What do we have to do? His Word states:

"Believe in the Lord Jesus Christ, and you WILL be saved..."

Acts 16:31

That alone is the key to salvation. Faith in Jesus Christ plus...NOTHING! This is SOOO hard! We have been conditioned to achieve, to throw our whole weight into a project or career. Try HARDER! Yet, the Eternal God, Creator of the Universe, says that no matter how hard we try, we cannot attain heaven by our own effort. We need a Savior! By faith we must receive Him. We then willingly choose to serve Him because we love Him. As a believer and disciple of Christ, each time as you take Communion, pause, remember, give thanks, and celebrate.

PRAYER

Lord Jesus, Your life is a most beautiful example for me to follow. Thank you for revealing my sin to me. I know that your death on the cross paid the price for my sin. The fact that You would take on flesh to save me, to reach me, causes me to praise You with all my heart and to serve you with my whole life. By faith in Your sacrifice, Your death, burial, and resurrection, my sins have been forgiven and washed away. I am a new creature in Christ. Help me to walk worthy of the wonderful gift of salvation you have given me. Thank you for your Holy Spirit who dwells in me. His presence is absolute proof that your promises are true. I am confident that You are going to guide me and direct me throughout my earthly life and then take me into your heavenly kingdom. In Jesus' Name, I thank You. Amen!

CHRIST IS IN ME! I AM IN CHRIST!

Can we grasp this incredible truth? When you trust in Christ as your Savior, He dwells IN you and is WITH you. Yes, when you believe and trust in Jesus Christ, He enters into your heart; He abides with you and in you.

> "Behold, I [Jesus] stand at the door and knock; if anyone hears My voice and opens the door, I will come in to him and will dine with him and he with Me."
>
> Revelation 3:20

He says He will never leave you or forsake you. Never! Never! **Never! Never!** When you take Communion, either at home or in public, He doesn't stay back in the seat and wait for you to finish. No! You are celebrating Him! When you take Communion, He celebrates with you and in you. You are remembering His life; His Spirit is WITH you and IN you. Jesus promised this in John 14: 16,17:

I will ask the Father, and He will give you another Helper, that He may be with you forever; that is the Holy Spirit of truth, whom the world cannot receive because it does not see Him or know Him, but you know Him because He abides **WITH** you and **IN** you.

PRAYER

Lord Jesus, thank You that You are always with me and dwell in me. You will never leave me or forsake me. As I partake of Communion, I remember the precious sacrifice You made to purchase my salvation. Thank You for paying the price for my sin and forgiving me. Thank You for giving me a hope and a future. Thank You for walking with me each day of my life and hearing me when I pray. I love You. I worship You in this special time as I meditate and remember who You are and all you have done for me. Do all You wish and desire in my life in any area you choose this day and every day.

"Christ IN me, the hope of glory."

Colossians 1:27

"If anyone is IN Christ, he is a new creature; the old things passed away; behold, new things have come."

II Corinthians 5:17

We celebrate the fact that as believers in Christ, our POSITION is that He (God) has "raised us up WITH Him, and seated us WITH Him in the heavenly places in Christ Jesus." (Ephesians 2:6) The Bible says that when we received Christ as our Savior we were instantly transferred from the kingdom of darkness to the kingdom of light, from the kingdom of Satan to the kingdom of God. Christ is IN us and we are IN Him. As we participate in Communion, His Spirit in us celebrates with us:

"Where two or three have gathered together in My Name, I am there in their midst."

Matthew 18:20

His presence makes our Communion experience even more meaningful, doesn't it? It is not just a piece of bread and a cup that we take with little or no reverence or forethought; it is a symbolic and active celebration of a living Christ who said, "Remember Me," and is present with us and in us.

We have all attended an awards ceremony for a loved one. When we are celebrating their tremendous victory and accomplishment, the person receiving the award is always present. The resurrection of Christ is the most important event in history. In its celebration at Communion, OF COURSE He would be present. It is His celebration of victory over sin and death. What a glorious thought! A beautiful intimacy transpires when we realize and know that as we remember Him at the Lord's Supper, He is with us and in us. What a wonderful reality! The incredible joy we have in our daily life is…

His Presence!

With the realization and awareness of His Presence in our lives each day, the Communion table becomes active, alive, and vibrant. It is no longer just ritual and tradition. Since I completed this study, I am overwhelmed each time I celebrate Communion, overwhelmed by His Presence more and more each day as I commune with Him. His unbelievable sacrifice for the human race was totally an act of love. His Spirit is in me. Think of it! The same Spirit that raised Christ from the dead is with me and in me. The same Holy Spirit that was present at His crucifixion and resurrection is present with me each day as I walk with Him, as I study His Word, and when I celebrate Communion. This is received by faith. Our small human minds can grasp only a portion of the magnitude of this:

"If the Spirit of Him who raised Jesus from the dead dwells IN you, He who raised Christ Jesus from the dead will give life to your mortal bodies through His Spirit who dwells in you."

Romans 8:11

PRAYER

"Oh Lord, when I repented of my sin and invited You into my heart, You came to dwell in me, to live with me. Your Holy Spirit has become my Guide, my precious Teacher. Your Word states that I have been sealed by the Holy Spirit, given to me as a pledge of my inheritance. As I take Communion, I welcome and rejoice in Your indwelling presence. Thank you that you are WITH me and IN me. In Jesus' Name, Amen!

WE PROCLAIM HIS DEATH UNTIL HE COMES

Jesus promised that He will complete the work that He began in us until the day of Christ Jesus…until He comes again. Christ promises us a hope and a future, an eternal life with Him. He is our coming King; He will return for His bride, the church, all those who are washed in the blood of the Lamb. In Chapter 11 of Corinthians, verse 26 we read:

> "As often as you eat this bread and drink the cup, you proclaim the Lord's death until He comes."
>
> I Corinthians 11:26

> "I go to prepare a place for you. If I go and prepare a place for you, I will come again and receive you to Myself that where I am, there you may be also."
>
> John 14:2b-3

Jesus is coming again. When? Friends, the end is near. All of the indications in the Scripture show that Christ could return any minute. Holy men and women of God even in the 1970's strongly believed that all of the Biblical signs were in place for Christ to return. That was FIFTY years ago. Are you ready today? As a disciple of Christ, each time we participate in Communion we proclaim, we herald, we boldly pronounce, we preach loudly to the world like a grand trumpet victory blast, the Lord's death until He comes. Communion is a powerful statement that Jesus is alive and well, and He is coming again; there will be peace and joy when the true King comes again to rule and to reign. There will be true peace on earth only when the Prince of Peace is on His throne.

Lord, Come Quickly!

Communion, instituted directly and personally by our Lord Jesus Christ, is an intimate, active, and vibrant celebration where we remember and rejoice in the entire work and Person of Jesus Christ. As we celebrate Communion, He said, "Remember Me": Remember My passionate love for you, what I did for you, why I took on human flesh, why I willingly chose to die on a cross and rise again. Remember that I am with you and in you as you partake, that I will never leave you or forsake you. I will complete the work that I began in you until the day of Christ Jesus. I will then come again and receive you to Myself. Where I am, you will be with Me also.

As a follower and disciple of Christ, He is with you and in you as you remember Him. As we study further, you will find it gets better and **better** and **BETTER** with even more blessings for you, available and received only by faith.

PRAYER

Oh Lord, how wonderful is Your work. I take Communion in celebration that You promised that You are coming again. I proclaim to the world that I am a child of God, my sins have been forgiven, that You will never leave me or forsake me and that You are coming again for me. You will rule and reign as King. Lord, come quickly.

As I meditated on His promises to return, my heart sang a new song; the words and melody flooded my mind. I then connected it to an old hymn, which I sing often, as I anxiously await His coming. I pray the words will be a blessing to you. I will spare you from my singing.

Maybe Today, Maybe Tonight

Maybe today, maybe tonight
My love will appear, make everything right
Maybe today, maybe tonight…I'll wait

Soon He'll appear, His face will I see
When He comes again
He's coming for me
Maybe today, maybe tonight…I'll wait

Glory, glory, joy to my heart He'll bring
Glory, glory, when we will crown Him King
Glory, glory, we will prepare the way
Glory, glory, Jesus will come someday

Maybe today, maybe tonight
I'll wait, I'll wait…He'll come!

CHRIST IS OUR PASSOVER?

Commentaries on the Bible give us exceptionally deep insight into the meaning of different passages and are the result of years of study by the authors. We have the privilege of reading and hearing the inspired truth of God and the opinion of the writer. However, the absolute best commentary on the Bible IS the Bible itself. When we examine a Scripture passage, other passages provide insight, wisdom, and clarity. In 1 Corinthians 5, we see not only a reference to the Lord's Supper and Communion but also a key to understanding its deeper significance with this incredible statement, "Christ our Passover also has been sacrificed." The following two verses reveal an eternal truth which greatly enhances our understanding:

> "For Christ our Passover also has been sacrificed.
> Therefore let us celebrate the feast, not with
> old leaven, nor with the leaven of malice and
> wickedness, but with the unleavened
> bread of sincerity and truth."
>
> I Corinthians 5: 7-8

Christ our Passover?

These two verses indicate that the Passover Feast of the Old Testament is connected to Communion, somehow being a representation of the Lord Jesus Christ. To understand the connection, we will examine many details of the Passover Celebration and see how they are a picture, or as the Apostle Paul says in Colossians, a "shadow" of Jesus Christ:

> Therefore no one is to act as your judge or in respect to a festival or a new moon or a Sabbath day – things which are a mere SHADOW of what is to come; but the substance [Literally: the body] belongs to Christ.
>
> Colossians 2: 16-17

The Mosaic feasts, rituals, and offerings of the Old Testament are each a shadow pointing to Jesus Christ and His ultimate sacrifice for the sins of humanity. As we look at different aspects of the Passover Feast, we will see that each characteristic is a picture of Christ, given true meaning by His life.

He is our Passover!

The Historical Setting of the Passover Feast

For more than 400 years, Israel was held in bondage and slavery in Egypt. God had raised up Moses as the Deliverer, the man who commanded Pharaoh to let God's people go. Pharaoh had resisted and hardened his heart time and again. In spite of the many plagues, he was unwilling to release the Israelites from bondage. The last plague from God was about to fall on Egypt. All of the first born of Egypt would be killed by the Angel of the Lord, "both man and beast" (see Exodus 12:12). In Exodus 12:3-10), Moses was given these instructions to save the Israelites:

> On the tenth of this month, they are each one to take a lamb for themselves, according to their fathers' households. Now if the household is too small for a lamb, then he and his neighbor nearest to his house are to take one according to the number of persons in them; according to what each man should eat, you are to divide the lamb. Your lamb shall be an unblemished male a year old; you may take it from the sheep or from the goats. You shall keep it until the fourteenth day of the same month, then the whole assembly of the congregation of Israel is to kill it at twilight. Moreover, they shall take some of the blood and put it on the two doorposts and on the lintel of the houses in which they eat it. They shall eat the flesh that same night, roasted with fire, and they shall eat it with unleavened bread and bitter herbs. Do not eat any of it raw or boiled at all with water, but rather roasted with fire, both its head and its legs along with its

entrails. And you shall not leave any of it over till morning, but whatever is left of it until morning, you shall burn with fire.

The blood of the lamb placed on the doorposts and the lintel (top) of the doorway caused the Death Angel to pass over the house. After the blood was placed on the door, what did they do with the flesh? They were commanded by God to eat it…to eat all of it with specific instructions:

"Now you shall eat of it in this manner: with your loins girded, your sandals on your feet, and your staff in your hand; and you shall eat it in haste -- it is the Lord's Passover."

Exodus 12:11

They were not to eat it any way they chose, with their own favorite recipe. Look at the detail of the commands regarding the flesh of the lamb:

- ✓ Eat it that same night
- ✓ Eat it roasted with fire and eaten with unleavened bread and bitter herbs
- ✓ Do not eat it raw or boiled at all with water
- ✓ Roast with fire, both its head and its legs along with its entrails

- ✓ Do not leave any of it over till morning
- ✓ Whatever is left over you shall burn with fire
- ✓ Eat it with your loins girded
- ✓ Eat it with your staff in your hand
- ✓ Eat it with your sandals on your feet
- ✓ Eat it in haste; it is the Lord's Passover

__Wait!__ The Passover is just the blood on the sides and on the top of the doorway, right? Isn't Communion only about the blood of Christ shed for our sins?

If that is correct, then why all of the specific instructions about the flesh, even that the bones of the lamb should not be broken? If both the blood and the flesh of the lamb were significant in the Passover Feast, then both are a "shadow" pointing to Christ, teaching us about Him. Because the New Testament states that "Christ is our Passover", several questions related to the Passover Feast now come to mind. Think carefully about each of these questions, even if it challenges your current beliefs. Our desire is the truth of the Word of God.

Reasonable Questions:

1. Why a spotless lamb, a male, without blemish?

2. Why was the lamb killed by the whole congregation?

3. What was the purpose of the blood?

4. Why was the blood put only on the doorposts and the lintel (top) and not on the threshold?

5. Why didn't they just throw the flesh of the lamb out, if it was of no significance, if only the blood was important?

6. Why were they instructed to prepare the flesh in a specific manner, even with commands regarding what they should wear?

7. Why is it important that none of the bones of the lamb be broken?

8. Why were they given careful commands not only to eat it, but to eat ALL of it?

If there is no significance in the flesh of the Passover lamb, why is there so much detail of what to do and what not to do? If the significance of the Passover was only the blood, then the passage inspired by the Holy Spirit in I Corinthians would state only **"Christ's blood is our Passover",** which would make the distinction and omit His body. But the passage clearly states that **"<u>Christ</u> is our Passover"**, causing us to look at the entire celebration with the Exodus account giving detailed instructions for both the blood and flesh of the lamb: how to prepare it, what to do with the blood, and what to do with the flesh of the lamb, and who are allowed to participate.

Is Christ our Passover, both the body AND the blood? We know the blood was for the forgiveness of sins, which is a vital aspect of every Communion service. What is the significance of the flesh as it relates to Christ? Looking at each part of the Passover Feast, let's see how both the blood and flesh of the lamb are a representation, a shadow pointing to Christ.

A Spotless Lamb

The Passover lamb had to be a one-year old lamb, without blemish and without spot, killed at twilight. The prophet Isaiah, Apostles Peter and John, all refer to Christ as the spotless Lamb:

> He was oppressed and He was afflicted, yet He did not open His mouth; Like **a lamb that is led to the slaughter**, And like a sheep that is silent before its shearers, So He did not open His mouth.
>
> Isaiah 53:7

"You were not redeemed with perishable things like
silver or gold from your futile way of life inherited
from your forefathers, but with **precious blood,
as of a lamb unblemished and spotless,**
the blood of Christ."

I Peter 1:18-19

"The next day he [John] saw Jesus coming to him and
said, "Behold, the **Lamb of God** who takes away
the sin of the world."

John 1:29

The Ethiopian Eunuch

In Acts 8:26-39, the Bible says an angel of the Lord spoke to Philip and told him to go south to the road that descends from Jerusalem to Gaza. When Philip arrived, he saw an Ethiopian eunuch, a court official of Candace, queen of the Ethiopians. He was sitting in his chariot reading the passage from the prophet Isaiah:

He was led as a sheep to the slaughter; and as a lamb before its shearer is silent, so He does not open His mouth. In humiliation His judgment was taken away; Who will relate His generation? For His life is removed from the earth.

From this account, we see that the eunuch invited Philip to join His chariot and explain the passage, asking, "Please tell me, of whom does the prophet say this? Of himself or someone else?" Philip, beginning from this Isaiah passage, preached Jesus to him, resulting in his conversion and baptism. These passages and numerous others distinctly show that the Passover lamb is a picture of Jesus, validating the claim that Christ is our Passover; the Passover Feast is a "shadow" of the true picture of Christ.

Killed at Twilight by the Entire Congregation

The spotless lamb was to be killed at twilight by the entire congregation, not by just a few people or a small group, but by the entire congregation. This is a symbolic picture of all humanity. There is no one born who is perfect and has no need of a Savior. No man can approach God on his own merits. When Adam sinned in the Garden of Eden, we all sinned in him. Romans 3:23 states:

"For all have sinned and fall short of the glory of God."

The entire human race is fallen and in need of a Savior. It was my sin and your sin that caused Christ to go to the cross.

The entire congregation at the Passover Feast was to kill the innocent lamb because all of us are guilty before a righteous and holy God, and all of us need a Savior. If only a portion of the congregation were to slay the lamb, the message sent would be that some people could make it to God on their own while others could not. The sacrifice of Christ was for all because everyone of us needs a Savior. Christ was arrested at twilight, in the evening, during Passover. The Passover Feast is a shadow; the real substance belonging to Christ.

No Broken Bones

When the Passover lamb was killed, the Jews were strictly commanded not to break any of its bones. (Exodus 12:46)

Messianic Prophecy in Psalms

"He keeps all his bones, not one of them is broken."

Psalm 34:20

Fulfillment in the New Testament

We have already established that Christ was referred to many times in the Old and New Testaments as the Lamb of God. When Christ was crucified with the two criminals, the Jews asked Pilate to have the legs of the criminals broken so they would die and the bodies would not be on the cross during the Sabbath. The soldiers broke the legs of the two men who were crucified with Christ, but when they came to Jesus, they saw that He was already dead so they did not break His legs. John states:

> Then the Jews, because it was the day of preparation, so that the bodies would not remain on the cross on the Sabbath (for that Sabbath was a high day), asked Pilate that their legs might be broken, and that they might be taken away. So the soldiers came and broke the legs of the first man and the other who was crucified with Him; but coming to Jesus, when they saw that He was already dead, they did not break His legs.
>
> John 19: 31-33

Coincidence?

No! A fulfillment of a Messianic prophecy! John clearly states in verse 36:

> "These things came to pass to fulfill the Scripture,
> 'NOT A BONE OF HIM SHALL BE BROKEN'."

Jesus Christ, our Passover, His body <u>and</u> His blood!

Who Could Celebrate the Passover?

In the Passover Feast, all of the congregation of Israel was commanded to celebrate it, but who was included in the phrase, "all of the congregation of Israel"?

> If a stranger sojourns with you, and celebrates the Passover to the Lord, let all his males be circumcised, and then let them come near to celebrate it; and he shall be like a native of the land. **But no uncircumcised person may eat of it.**
>
> Exodus 12:48

Not everyone in Israel was permitted to celebrate the Passover. The condition was they had to be Jewish or "like a native in the land", which meant, circumcised. One who was not circumcised was not allowed to take the Passover. However, circumcision in the New Testament Covenant was not physical; it was of the heart by faith in Christ, as stated by the Apostle Paul in Colossians 2: 11-12:

> In Him [Christ] you were also circumcised with a circumcision made without hands, in the removal of the body of the flesh by the circumcision of Christ, having been buried with Him in baptism, in which you were also raised up with Him through faith in the working of God, who raised Him from the dead."

Later, we will examine more closely as to who should or should not take Communion, and you will see that there are specific Scriptural conditions concerning participation in the blessings of Communion just as there were concerning the Passover Feast. We should know and expect to receive by faith all of the blessings in Christ and celebrate them by taking Communion in the proper manner. We should also want to know any commands that might cause us to examine ourselves and decide NOT to take Communion, shouldn't we?

How to Eat the Passover and What to Wear

Again, what difference does it make? If we are only concerned with the blood of the Passover lamb, why so many details about the flesh? And even what to wear:

> "Now you shall eat of it in this manner: with your
> loins girded, your sandals on your feet,
> and your staff in your hand; and you shall
> eat it in haste -- it is the Lord's Passover."

> Exodus 12:11

In our study thus far, we are gradually laying the foundation for a detailed study of Communion as taught in I Corinthians 11, showing that it is far, far more than just a ritual, but that it has deep, rich, meaning relating to the complete sacrifice of Jesus Christ for you and me. As the church in Berea, please study this next passage carefully as it is profoundly eye-opening as to the significance of His being scourged and beaten prior to His crucifixion.

THE FLESH OF THE LAMB, THE BODY OF CHRIST

Most of the Communion services I have participated in are focused primarily on His shed blood for the forgiveness of our sin. *"What can wash away my sin, nothing but the blood of Jesus!"* We can never overemphasize His shed blood. However, prior to His blood He brings attention to His body and makes it a vital part of the Communion celebration. Yet, almost never do we hear teaching related to the body of Christ being broken for us. Why not? Scripture is very clear on the significance of His body and His blood. As we move into this important section be open-minded and search the Scripture carefully to see if what is written is true.

We now further validate our claim of Christ being our Passover, represented by both the flesh and the blood of the lamb. Isaiah 53: 4, 5 is plainly a prophetic passage about the coming Messiah, explaining the sacrifice of our Lord:

Surely *our* **griefs** He Himself bore, And our **sorrows** He carried; Yet we ourselves esteemed Him stricken, Smitten of God and afflicted. But He was pierced through for our transgressions, He was crushed for our iniquities; the chastening for our well-being fell upon Him, And by His **scourging** we are **healed.**

Let's look closely at the translation of the key underlined words, referring to the original language from *The New Strong's Expanded Exhaustive Concordance of the Bible:*

Griefs: "2483: malady (a disease or ailment), anxiety, calamity: -- sickness (12x), disease (7x), grief (4x), sick (1)" (Strong, 2001b, p.89).

Sorrows : "4341: anguish or (fig.) affliction:--grief (2x), pain (2x), sorrow (12x)" (Strong, 2001b, p.157).

The original language of Hebrew illuminates the translation further and allows us to begin to understand the tremendous sacrificial work of Christ.

"Surely our **griefs** [malady, disease, ailment, anxiety, calamity, sickness, grief] He Himself bore, and our **sorrows** [anguish, affliction, grief, pain, sorrow] He carried."

Yes, Jesus died for our sins, but there is more to His sacrifice then the forgiveness of our sins. There was a purpose for both the body and the blood of our Lord, both understood in the Passover Feast. There is a clear connection to our healing. But what does that mean?

By His scourging, by His <u>stripes</u>, we are <u>healed</u>. Let's return again to the original language regarding the Hebrew word for "stripes, scourging" and also the word for "healed".

Stripes, Scourging: "2250: i.e. a weal (or black and blue mark itself):-- stripe (3x), hurt (1x), wounds (1x), blueness (1x), bruise (1x)" (Strong, 2001b, p.79).

Healed: "7495 rapha, *raw-faw'*: to mend (by stitching), i.e. (fig.) to cure: --heal (57x), physician (5x), cure (1x), repaired (1x), misc. (3x) = X thoroughly, make whole. (1) Rapah means to heal, a restoring to normal" (Strong, 2001b, p.265).

We are healed by His stripes (wounds)? The scourging of Jesus had the inclusive purpose of our healing including physical, mental, and emotional sicknesses and pains? How else can Isaiah 53 be explained? Without ignoring the text, what other implication would it suggest? Jesus Christ's death on the cross had healing in every area for us...spiritual, physical, mental, and emotional. He is a complete Savior, a complete Healer, able to make us thoroughly whole. Is the Bible truly saying that the beating, scourging, and crucifixion of Jesus Christ has benefits for all of who we are physically, emotionally, mentally, and spiritually? Can we find validation in the New Testament? Virtually all of the commentaries say, "No!" But the best commentary on the Bible is the Bible itself. A study of the original languages points to the fact that we have greatly limited and minimized the wonderful work of Christ on the cross only to His shed blood for the forgiveness of our sins. By faith ONLY in His blood, the full blessing of Christ's work for you is not appropriated.

Is there New Testament Validation?

Yes! This is something wonderful the Lord wants us to know, to believe by faith in our daily walk with, Him and to celebrate in the Communion service. This is an amazing aspect of our Lord's death that has been largely overlooked by the church causing us to miss and not appropriate the full blessing He has for us. Why? Because we have not been properly taught, and therefore, we do not believe. If we do not believe, we cannot and will not receive. However, that's about to change for you, releasing new blessings in your life, through faith in Christ.

Slow Down…Don't Move TOO Fast!

Now, at this point in time let's resolve not to go too fast and too far in our thinking. The subject of healing is very complex and varied. We all know many good people who have been very ill and died, young and old. We all know some who have recovered almost miraculously, instantly, gradually, and through use of the wonderful blessings God has provided through our healthcare professionals. Individuals very close to us have prayed for years to be healed and have not been. God is Sovereign. Why are some healed and some not? I have the perfect answer for you. **I don't know.**

However, that does not minimize what the Bible says just because we don't have an actual answer for every situation. At this time, let's take baby steps and not gigantic predetermined leaps based on what we believe and have seen from our own experience. The question before us is one and one only:

Is there healing provided for us in Christ that is appropriated by faith in His scourging, death, burial, resurrection, and ascension?

Before you cry out, **"NO!"**, read on and consider new information from the Bible:

> When Jesus came into Peter's home, He saw his mother-in-law lying sick in bed with a fever. He touched her hand, and the fever left her; and she got up and waited on Him. When evening came, they brought to Him many who were demon-possessed, and He cast out the spirits with a word, and healed all who were ill. <u>This was to fulfill what was spoken through Isaiah the prophet: "He Himself took our infirmities [weakness and sickness of the body and of the soul] and carried away our diseases.</u>

This passage in Matthew 8: 14-17, tells of many who were demon-possessed and were brought to Jesus. He cast out the spirits with a word and then healed all who were ill (sick and diseased). Matthew, moved by the Holy Spirit, writes that this was to fulfill the prophecy in Isaiah, stating that the death of Christ on the cross was for the entire human condition. If we examine other cases of demon-possession in passages of the Gospels, we can clearly see examples of physical, mental, emotional, and spiritual illnesses that were healed by Christ. He is a complete Savior. In the United States, we focus almost primarily on the fact that the blood of Jesus cleanses us from all sin.

Communion remembers His death and His blood that washed away my sin, that He took the penalty for my sin and bled and died that I might live. But what about His Body? We have entirely neglected what the Scripture states. An accurate study of Isaiah lends strong support and proof to the position that His body was scourged for our complete healing.

If you are willing to deny this, then you are claiming that Matthew, speaking by the Spirit of God, is mistaken when he states that Christ healed all who were sick and diseased and that this was to fulfill the Isaiah prophecy. To deny this is to deny the correct meaning of the translation in Isaiah 53. If His death was only for the forgiveness of sin and spiritual healing, then He would have delivered the demon-possessed only and turned away all who were physically ill.

Dr. Michael Brown, (2005), a Messianic Jew, in a series of tapes on divine healing, states that it is unheard of in Middle Eastern cultures that salvation and healing were only for the soul, but the body was allowed to remain sick. He states that even in the false religions, healing was always spoken of for the entire person…body, soul, and spirit. He has an excellent audio series entitled, *I Am the Lord Your Healer.* Tape 2 of the series explains the deep significance of *"rapha"*, the Hebrew word for complete healing in all areas of our life (https://www.AskDrBrown.org). In America, we usually focus only on a person being saved spiritually, but ignore the body.

Why then was Jesus scourged, beaten beyond recognition? Why would He receive the lashes of the brutal Roman scourging and not say a word? For no reason? Would God allow this merciless beating of Christ just for fun? No! Isaiah states that His stripes, that His scourging had a purpose…our healing in all areas including mental, emotional, spiritual, and physical. Jesus, the entire God-man, gave His entire being for the complete deliverance of the entire human condition…body, soul, and spirit. Hallelujah! Amen! The Lord be magnified! If I haven't yet convinced you that there is healing in the body and the blood of Christ for you, stay tuned as the Scripture gives us even further validation.

Chuck Smith, the late pastor of Calvary Chapel in California, details the horrible scourging process of the Romans in his teaching on Matthew 27:26:

"Then he [Pilate] released Barabbas for them; but
after having Jesus scourged, he handed
Him over to be crucified."

Now scourging before crucifixion was common Roman practice. The prisoner would be tied to a post in such a way, in such a position, that his back would be bent over. And then the Roman guard would take a leather whip in which there were bits of bone, and pieces of lead imbedded. And over the stretched back, the prisoner of course was stripped naked, and over his back, he would lay this whip, which as he would pull it back would pick up pieces of flesh with it, with these little bits of lead and bone embedded in the whip. The prisoners oftentimes died at the whipping post. Most generally they fainted two or three times during the beating.

The purpose of the scourging was to solve the unsolved crimes in the community. The idea being that if the prisoner would confess to a crime, that the executioner applying the whip would make it a little easier each time. But if he was stubborn and refused to confess some crime against Rome, then he lay it on harder, and harder, and harder until the prisoner, because of excruciating pain, was forced to cry out his crimes against Rome.

They always had a man standing by, a scribe, ready to write down the things that the prisoner confessed. And thus, the Roman government was able to solve many of the crimes in the community by this method of torture. Again, "as a sheep before her shearers is dumb, so He opened not His mouth."

He had absolutely nothing to confess. The sentence was forty stripes, for forty is the number of judgment in the Scriptures. However, there would be only thirty-nine stripes laid upon the prisoner, thirty-nine being the number of mercy, not much mercy... not much mercy.

But to show mercy, the Roman government would only lay on thirty-nine, though forty was always the sentence. Many times the prisoner would bleed to death, having received the scourging, they would be physically weakened, their backs torn to shreds, looking like hamburger. (Smith, 1982-85)

This is not something that God would lay on Christ, or that Christ would willingly receive for absolutely no reason. Christ Himself, in Matthew 8, states that it had a healing purpose. Isaiah states that it had a healing purpose. To even suggest or think that there was no purpose to the scourging is to deny Scripture and to infer that God the Father is a cruel taskmaster, flaying Christ's flesh into a gory mess for no reason whatsoever... the act of a merciless, cruel, unloving Father.

Further New Testament Validation

In 1 Peter 2 we see a very interesting verse we should investigate:

"And He Himself bore our sins in His body on the cross,
so that we might die to sin and live to righteousness;
for by His wounds you **_were_ healed**."

This word for "healed" is a Greek word. Let's refer to Strong's concordance for the original meaning which is quite remarkable.

Healed: "2390: to cure (lit. or fig.):--heal (26x), make whole (2x)." (Strong, 2001a, p. 119) Throughout the Old Testament, it is used both of physical treatment <u>and</u> spiritual healing. James 5:16 possibly includes both (Strong, 2001a, p.119).

The <u>same passage in Isaiah 53</u> is referred to by Peter, but with a slightly different emphasis. By His stripes you <u>WERE</u> healed, past tense. This passage creates new questions, stating that our healing in Christ, also due to His scourging, was already accomplished at the cross over 2000 years ago; we now appropriate it by faith when we receive Christ as our Savior and continually throughout our daily walk with Him.

I heard a well-known minister wrongly say, "No person who believes in divine healing will EVER quote this passage in 1 Peter because it is not referring to physical healing." We are quoting its relevance here. The context in this passage is that the purpose of His stripes was so that we might "die to sin and live to righteousness" referring to spiritual healing, the forgiveness of our sin. The passage in Matthew refers to spiritual, physical, mental, and emotional healing as He healed all who were ill. Can we separate the body, the soul, and the spirit? Quite frankly, the message we can easily understand from the combination of both passages in Matthew and 1 Peter is not to rule out one or the other, but to show the completeness of the sacrifice of the whole person of Jesus Christ for the whole person of me…body, soul, and spirit. It causes me to know that there is a deep, wonderful mystery to the work that Christ did for us. Isaiah and Matthew say that by His stripes we ARE healed. Peter states, after the resurrection of Christ, by His stripes you WERE healed. When did our healing happen? At the cross! Your healing is already complete in Christ. Many limit the healing of Christ to spiritual only, but this is not consistent with what the Scripture plainly states. In Isaiah, how can we explain away that He carried our disease, sickness, and our pains, our anxiety, sorrow, and grief? Was His scourging uncontrolled by God? Was it meaningless? Why couldn't He shed His blood without the beating?

God is NOT a sadist, just allowing Christ to receive the brutal Roman beating for no reason whatsoever, just for fun. Christ stated that He had the power to lay His life down and to take it up again. Do you believe our glorious Savior would give Himself to the beatings, the crown of thorns, and the scourging for no reason whatsoever? No, the scourging was for our emotional, mental, physical, and spiritual healing, as was His blood for the forgiveness of our sins. Jesus Christ died a cruel death for all of humanity, giving Himself, all of His body and blood for all of me, for all of you, for all of mankind, whoever believes on His Name, that we might be reconciled back to God…the perfect sacrifice.

Divine Healing?

I know full well what you are thinking. I am thinking and praying through the same questions. If the scourging of Christ was for our healing in all areas, then why isn't everyone who believes in Him healed? Why are many still sick? I agree with you that these are very difficult and complex questions that I do not fully understand and probably never will this side of heaven. A bit more light will be shed on this subject with more of an in-depth study on 1 Corinthians 11, which we will undertake in the upcoming chapter on "Discerning, Judging the Body". In my journey through these questions and my study of His Word, He gives me more and more light into these issues, which may result in a more detailed publication at a later time. Regardless, I will not and cannot take away from or modify His Word just because it is difficult to explain or understand. Search each of the Scriptures for yourself and ask the Holy Spirit to give you wisdom and insight. I have looked at the original languages in each of the passages and cannot explain them away. However, just because you and I don't fully understand them, does not mean they are not true. I urge you to take off "rose colored" glasses and pre-determined conclusions, and please give an honest, objective view of what the Scripture is proclaiming. The benefit will be yours as you correctly appropriate the complete work that Jesus Christ accomplished for you.

I can honestly and personally attest to the following five truths about healing, having validated it with the Word of God and, by faith, personally experienced its truths with self and others. Are you ready?

1. I have both personally experienced and seen instant, miraculous, complete healing through prayer, sometimes to the amazement and wonder of the physician.

2. I have seen healing to be partial or gradual. Christ did not always heal the individual immediately.

3. I have seen the tremendous skill and God-given gifts of surgeons, physicians, nurses, healthcare professionals, and holistic practitioners utilized in the healing process. Thank God, pray for them, and ask God for wisdom in the proper utilization of their services.

4. I have seen the power of Christ dramatically change people, restore marriages, deliver from drug addiction, suicidal thoughts, pornography and all sorts of mental, physical, emotional, spiritual, and even financial woes. He came that we might have life...abundant life. Here!

5. I have seen, for reasons known only to the Sovereign God, wonderful, good, and godly persons pray and pray for healing for years and end up leaving this earthly life. But I know this...God is good, and God is righteous and just...always!

Consider the command for sickness given to the church in James 5:13-16, regarding all types of healing needs. Let's be reasonable. If no one is EVER going to get sick, there is no reason God would give us this command:

Is anyone among you suffering? Then he must pray. Is anyone cheerful? He is to sing praises. Is anyone among you sick? Then he must call for the elders of the church and they are to pray over him, anointing him with oil in the name of the Lord; and the prayer offered in faith will restore the one who is sick, and the Lord will raise him up, and if he has committed sins, they will be forgiven him. Therefore, confess your sins to one another, and pray for one another so that you may be healed.

This, of course, is worthy of a deeper, longer discussion which will not be undertaken here.

Friends, we are commanded not to add or take away from Scripture. Often, to take away from Scripture is just to omit part of it, explain it away, or modify it to fit our pre-determined belief, even if our belief is false. No one who is a disciple and follower of Jesus Christ will deny that the precious blood of our Lord was shed for the forgiveness of our sins. This is what we celebrate as we take Communion, but why are we ignoring and not explaining the significance of the Body of our Lord, the scourging that He endured for us? How then do we explain that the passage in Peter relates His scourging to the penalty for sin, which is always said to be only the blood, yet the passage in Matthew relates the scourging to include the body as well as mental and emotional issues. The sacrifice for our sin and all aspects of our healing was not just the blood, not just the body. The complete sacrifice was the entire Person of the...

LORD JESUS CHRIST!

Both the body and the blood of Christ, all of Him should be the vital focus of our life and our Communion celebration, as we shall see. To eliminate the body, or ignore it, is stated by Paul as "not judging the body correctly", which has unfortunate consequences.

As we return to I Corinthians 11, we will see that Paul gets even more serious about both the body and the blood of Christ, making sure we understand, receive, and appropriate by faith the full benefits of the sacrifice of Jesus Christ for us.

THE GLORIOUS COMMUNION CELEBRATION
1 Corinthians 11: 23 - 33

Once we fully embrace and believe in the complete work of Christ as truly taught in the Bible, it will birth in us a new celebration of joy as we faithfully receive each day all the benefits Christ paid for us. With a deeper understanding of Communion, our participation will be an active, exciting experience. Why? Because as believers and disciples, Jesus Christ is with us and in us. He will minister to us in different ways based on our needs at that time. Let's look specifically at the main Communion passage:

Verses 23,24:

> For I received from the Lord that which I also delivered to you, that the Lord Jesus in the night in which He was betrayed took bread; and when He had given thanks, He broke it and said. 'This is My body, which is for you; do this in remembrance of Me'.

The Apostle says he received it directly from the Lord Jesus and is commanded to deliver it. Jesus took the bread and gave thanks, then he broke it. The bread was symbolic of His body. His body, which the Bible says is "**for you**". This is a reference to His living, fleshly body. As He broke the bread, He was in the flesh at that time, seated with His disciples, so the bread was just bread, not a piece of His body. The scourging and brutal beating was for us; it had a divine purpose, a vital part of the Lord's Supper.

<u>Verse 25:</u>

> In the same way He took the cup also after supper, saying, 'This cup is the new covenant in My blood; do this, as often as you drink it, in remembrance of Me'.

He then took the cup, a symbol of His blood that was going to be shed to pay the price for the sins of humanity, making peace with God through the cross. A NEW Covenant…in His blood. All of the "shadows" of the feasts and rituals in the Old Testament pointed to the one final sacrifice…the precious Son of God. We have peace with God through faith in the shed blood of Jesus Christ for our sins.

<u>Verse 26:</u>

> For as often as you <u>eat this bread and drink this cup</u>, you proclaim the Lord's death till He comes."

Both elements of the Communion celebration are incredibly significant…His body and His blood. As our Lord commanded, we do both…<u>eat this bread AND drink this cup.</u> In the Communion service we remember and celebrate His life death, burial, resurrection, and ascension. We praise Him that we have salvation, and we have been reconciled back to God. Through Jesus Christ, we now have peace with God. As often as we eat the bread and drink the cup, we are proclaiming that we believe in the finished work of Jesus Christ, and we are boldly proclaiming we are His and we await His return. He is coming again, not as a baby in a manger, not to be scourged, beaten, and crucified, not to pay the penalty for sin. He is coming as King and Judge of the world. But…before you take Communion…there are conditions!

There Are Conditions?

Is that, like, rules? Yes, 1 Corinthians 11:27 states clear conditions for being involved in the Communion celebration.

Over the years, the common practice I have seen is that everyone and anyone takes Communion, an ocean with no boundaries that becomes a swamp, with little or no instruction to the participants. However, to broaden the Communion service to allow everyone, men, women, and children of all ages to participate has serious consequences, according to the Scripture. The Communion service seen in most churches has been watered down horribly, to our detriment, but perhaps not intentionally. Let's turn again to the original language for clarification of three words: unworthy, guilty and examine.

<u>Verse 27, 28:</u>

> Therefore whoever eats the bread or drinks the cup of the Lord in an **unworthy** manner, shall be **guilty** of the body and the blood of the Lord. But a man must **examine** himself, and in so doing he is to eat of the bread and drink of the cup."

Unworthy: "371: irreverently(2x):--unworthily(2x), i.e., treating it as a common meal, the bread and the cup as common things, not apprehending their solemn, symbolic import" (Strong, 2001a, p.22).

Guilty: "1777: liable to (a condition, penalty or imputation):-- in danger of (5x), guilty of (4x), subject to (1x)." (Strong, 2001a, p. 89).

Examine: "1381: to test (lit. or fig.) by imp. to approve:– prove (10x), try (4x), approve (3x), discern (2x), allow (2x), like (1x), examine (1x)" (Strong,2001a, p. 71).

In the Passover Feast, not everyone was allowed to take part in the celebration, as we discussed on page 62. I know in our modern society that we do not like boundaries; we do not like rules or conditions, being told we cannot or should not do something. However, when it is the Lord Jesus Christ giving us the condition, wouldn't it be wise to take heed? If you examine yourself based on your relationship with Jesus Christ, according to the Scripture as stated by Paul, you will be able to self-determine whether you should or should not take Communion. Your relationship to Jesus Christ is the standard of measure.

Who is Jesus to You?

Is He your Savior? Your Lord and Master? Have you realized your fallen condition before a holy God and chosen to turn your life over to Him, receive and follow Him? After you understand this one condition and determine that you do not meet it and you still choose to take Communion anyway, Paul, directed by the Lord Jesus Christ Himself, says you are guilty of the body and the blood of the Lord, treating the sacrifice of Christ's death on the cross as trivial. You may have never been instructed of this, but now you are. You can honestly examine yourself and make the best decision…for you. Because the conditions come directly from the Lord Jesus Christ, I am quite sure they are non-negotiable and therefore, you should know them.

If the expectation to enter the presence of God is 100% purity and holiness, who can be worthy? The answer is easy…

No One!

"For <u>ALL</u> have sinned and fall short of the glory of God!"

Romans 3:23

"There is none righteous, not even one; There is none who understands, There is none who seeks for God."

Romans 3:10 - 11

> If we say that we have no sin, we are deceiving ourselves and the truth is not in us. If we confess our sins, He is faithful and just to forgive us our sins and to cleanse us from all unrighteousness. If we say that we have not sinned, we make Him a liar and His word is not in us
>
> I John 1: 8-10

If you or anyone is good enough to make it to heaven and able to live a perfect life, there was no need for Christ to die for our sins. Everyone would agree that there are many, many individuals doing good, moral deeds. Typically, we establish our own measure of goodness by comparing ourselves to others. We love to justify ourselves by placing ourselves above others. Unfortunately, that is the wrong comparison. The Sermon on the Mount in Matthew 5:48 states that we are to "be perfect as our heavenly Father is perfect!" Who can stand?

Only One, Jesus the Christ!

The wonderful news is that by faith in Christ, His righteousness is imputed to us. God sees us through the righteousness of Christ. Our sin was placed on Him. In Christ, **you are worthy.** Christ in you is the hope of glory! When you place your faith in the saving work of Christ, He forgives you of all your sin, wipes your slate clean, and comes to dwell in you by His Holy Spirit. He makes you worthy because He is worthy. Without a relationship with Christ, according to Scripture, you cannot be worthy. Stay with me on this. It is not to exclude...but to **include** you. You must come to God only through His way, the ONE and ONLY way...Jesus Christ!

The Blood Was Not Put on the Threshold

The blood of the Passover Lamb was put on the side of the door and the lintel (top). It was not put on the threshold. None of the children of Israel were to step on the blood. To examine yourself and know that you have not received Jesus Christ as Savior, and then to choose to take Communion anyway is taking Communion in an unworthy manner, because you cannot be worthy by your own good deeds. You cannot come to God by any method you choose.

> How much severer punishment do you think he will deserve who has trampled underfoot the Son of God, and has regarded as unclean the blood of the covenant by which he was sanctified, and has insulted the Spirit of grace?"
>
> Hebrews 10:29

I know this sounds extremely harsh, but which of you, if you KNOW that the Lord Himself, the AUTHOR of Communion, states that you are eating and drinking guilt to yourself, would want to proceed? Why? If you know it is against His direct command, and He is cautioning you for good reason, for your own personal good, to keep you from judgment, then you are doing better for yourself by NOT taking Communion. I freely confess that I do not completely understand what it means when the Bible says a person can be "guilty of the body and the blood of Christ", but it doesn't sound good or something that I desire for you or me .

You have the freedom and the right to believe whatever you choose, but this caution is directly from the Apostle Paul who states that He received it "from the Lord", the Lord who INSTITUTED the Communion celebration.

What's the Point?

God is holy! He desires to passionately have relationship with you, but because He is perfectly holy and we are not, we MUST approach Him HIS way. No man or woman can come to God on his or her own merits:

"For by grace you have been saved through faith; and
that <u>NOT of yourselves</u>, it is a gift of God;
<u>not as a result of works, that no man may boast."</u>

Ephesians 2: 8-9

"Nothing in my hands I bring
Simply to Thy cross I cling,
Naked, come to Thee for rest,

Helpless, look to Thee for grace,
Foul, I to the mountain fly.
Wash me, Savior, or I die."

Rock of Ages, Verse 2

To enter into the presence of God, the sin problem has to be addressed. In the Mosaic Law, for the Jewish people, the blood of bulls and goats atoned for (covered) their sin. The way to approach God in the New Covenant, instituted by the Lord Himself, is not by good works, sacrifices, or burnt offerings...it is by the blood of Jesus Christ...ONLY! Salvation and eternal life are based on faith in Jesus Christ plus NOTHING! No work of your hands can get you any closer to heaven. There is no 51%. You are commanded to examine yourself. If you have not believed in the work and person of Christ and have not received Him as your Lord and Savior, you should willingly and honestly, before God, choose **not** to take Communion…for your own benefit. <u>Note that this is NOT God's desire, and it is NOT mine.</u> He desires to have relationship with you through Jesus Christ, desiring all men and women to be saved and to come to a knowledge of Him:

> "The Lord is not slow about His promise [to return],
> as some count slowness, but is patient toward you,
> not wishing for any to perish but for
> ALL to come to repentance."
>
> 2 Peter 3:9

> "Precious in the sight of the Lord
> Is the death of His godly ones."
>
> Psalm 116:15

> "'As I live!' declares the Lord God, 'I take no pleasure in the
> death of the wicked, but rather that the wicked
> turn from his way and live.'"
>
> Ezekiel 33:11

My message is NOT to have you exclude yourself from taking Communion, to leave you out; it is to invite you to receive the wonderful news of the Gospel. No matter what you have done, how bad or good a life you have lived…the Eternal

God the Father, Creator of the Universe LOVES YOU and desires a relationship with you through Christ.

> God so loved the world, that He gave His only begotten Son, that whosoever believes in Him [insert your name] should not perish, but have eternal life. For God did not send the Son into the world to judge [condemn] the world, but that the world might be saved through Him.
>
> John 3:16-17

The arms of God are open wide to receive you, to forgive you of all your sins and welcome you as a son or a daughter, accepted, forgiven, and at peace with God. Jesus Christ became your Substitute. Please do not EXCLUDE yourself, **INCLUDE** yourself by coming into a loving relationship with God through the shed blood of Christ. Do not believe those who say there is another way! Jesus Christ is the ONLY way! After 40 years of serving Him, I am able to testify that He is the way, the truth and the life, as He said. Christ will come into your heart and dwell with you and in you. He will give you a peace that you have never known. With a sincere prayer of repentance and acceptance of Jesus Christ, you will be instantly transferred from the kingdom of darkness to the kingdom of light, from the kingdom of Satan to the kingdom of God. As a new child of

God, you can willingly come to the Communion celebration, knowing that in Christ you are worthy.

I Invite You to Receive Christ. Here! Now!

With a simple, childlike prayer, Christ will forgive you of your sins and come into your heart and life. He will bridge the gap between you and your loving Father God and change your life. It doesn't matter how many mistakes you have made, or how you have messed up. God LOVES you and wants a relationship with you. He will take all of your broken pieces and put them back together.

"A broken heart I gave, a worthless thing
An empty life was all that I could bring
Then Jesus filled my life with love divine.
He healed my broken heart, now I know
He's mine."

Pray With Me

Lord Jesus, I believe You died on the cross as a Substitute for all of my sins. Please forgive me of my sins, save me, and come into my heart. By faith I receive You as my Lord, (Master) and Savior. Help me to live a life that is pleasing to You, to learn Your commands and follow You closely. Thank you, Jesus, for saving me and forgiving me.

If you just prayed this prayer, receive His salvation by faith and thank Him. Many years ago, on the edge of suicide, I prayed a similar prayer. I didn't see flashes of lightning and thunder. I didn't feel much of anything. In the black darkness of my sad heart, desiring a reason and purpose for life, I heard four distinct, new words emanating from within the deepest part of my being, as if a single candle was lit. Coming from the lips of the Savior, He said personally to me:

I LOVE YOU!
LIVE!

"Therefore if anyone is in Christ, he is
a new creature; the old things passed away
behold, new things have come."
2 Corinthians 5:17

DISCERNING, JUDGING THE BODY

Let's dig deeper into the passage. If you are in Christ and wish to celebrate Communion, then there are additional, wonderful benefits for you which you may not previously have realized or experienced. We want you to experience and appropriate ALL of them. Let's continue with 1 Corinthians 11: 23-33:

Verse 29:

> For he who eats and drinks, eats and drinks judgment to himself if he does not judge the body rightly. For this reason many among you are weak and sick, and a number sleep."

You are the one who is responsible before God to examine your heart and make the decision to take or not take the bread and the cup. Those who are teachers have the duty to properly inform you correctly concerning what the Bible says and then allow you to examine yourself.

By faith, we drink the cup remembering His blood that was shed for the forgiveness of our sins. By faith, we take the bread signifying His body that was broken for our healing, our diseases, and sicknesses, physically, mentally, emotionally and spiritually. Those who are in Christ can eat and drink judgment to themselves by NOT discerning the BODY rightly…read carefully…**not the blood, but the body.**

If you examine the Scripture and you do NOT believe that His body was broken for your sicknesses, diseases and pain, then the benefits and blessings of His Body cannot be imparted or enjoyed by you, as they must be received by faith. Let's take a closer look at verses 29 and 30.

Verse 29:
> "For he who eats and drinks, eats and drinks judgment to himself if <u>he does not judge the body rightly</u>."

Ok, so what? I didn't judge the body correctly.

Verse 30:
> "For this reason many among you are <u>weak and sick and a number sleep.</u>"

Why? Because of a lack of knowledge and faith, they did not discern (judge) the body correctly. Let's again look at the meanings in the original language:

Weak: "770; to be feeble (in any sense):- be weak (12x), be sick (10x), sick (7x), weak (3x), be diseased (1x), impotent man (1x), be made weak (1x). This word means lit., lacking strength, weakness, infirmity" (Strong, 2001a, p. 44).

Sick: "732: infirm:-- sick (2x), sick folk (1x), be sick (1x), sickly (1x). This word means 'feeble, sickly'" (Strong, 2001a, p. 732).

> **Sleep:** 2837: to put to sleep, i.e. (pass or ref.) to slumber; fig. to decease:--sleep (10x), fall asleep (4x), be asleep (2x), be dead (1x). (7) This metaphorical use of the word sleep is appropriate, because of the similarity in appearance between a sleeping body and a dead body; restfulness and peace normally characterize both. As the sleeper does not cease to exist while his body sleeps, so the dead person continues to exist despite his absence from the region in which those who remain can communicate with him, and that, as sleep is known to be temporary, so the death of the body will be found to be. (Strong, 2001a, p.141)

The context of this verse regarding judging the body is referring to Christians. This is not a message of condemnation but a beautiful message of hope. Christ forgave you of your sins, but there is also healing in the cross. Christ did not undergo a terrible scourging for no reason at all. You are able to receive spiritual, physical, mental, and emotional healing even as you take Communion. Again, healing can be instant, or gradual. God is sovereign. By faith, be open to receiving everything God has for you. Regarding any needed healing, please <u>do not be foolish and ignore or remove yourself</u> from the expert work and wisdom God has given our healthcare professionals, especially if you are under their care:

> "Where there is no guidance the people fall,
> But in abundance of counselors there is victory."

> Proverbs 11:14

By faith receive the total finished work of Christ for forgiveness of your sins and any need you may have in any area of your life. He is a complete Savior. Celebrate Him! Paul states that Christians, by not judging (discerning) the body correctly, are weak (physically weak, feeble), sick (without strength, feeble, sickly) and a multitude sleep, which means they have died.

Now, if we are not to add or take away from God's Word, what should we do with this verse? Paul, by the Spirit, is saying that some do not discern the body correctly. By not discerning the body correctly and receiving it by faith, they have accepted and perhaps "opened themselves" to sickness, weakness, feebleness and even possibly early death. What is it about His blood AND His body that would protect and possibly prevent sickness, feebleness and even early death? Paul, speaking by the Holy Spirit states it...**Faith!** Faith is discerning and believing in the complete, finished work of Christ for you, both His body and His blood. Jesus Christ died so that you could be made whole physically, mentally, emotionally, and spiritually. He is a complete Savior.

Let's read again part of a message from Chuck Smith, the late pastor of Calvary Chapel, that relates to this section of 1 Corinthians.

"As a lamb before her shearers is dumb, so He opened not His mouth" (Isaiah 53: 7). Pilate scourged Jesus. He had laid upon Him thirty-nine lashes or stripes. This was no accident. This was something that was prophesied in the book of Isaiah, when Isaiah prophesied of His death. He said, "He was wounded for our transgressions, He was bruised for our iniquity. The chastisement of our peace is upon Him, and with His stripes we are healed" (Isaiah 53:5). So through the broken body of Christ we were healed. He suffered for us. So that he who eats of the body of Christ not discerning the Lord's body does not take and receive that healing provided for us through the suffering of Jesus. And for this cause a lot of people are sick, a lot of people are weak; and some have even died. You could have been healed if you had only appropriated the work of Jesus. But they have not discerned the Lord's body when they took the broken bread.

I think there is a lot of validity to this position. There are those who object to it, but I really feel that an honest evaluation of the Scriptures does lend a lot of validity to that position. I personally take it. I believe that there are a lot of people who could be healed if they would just appropriate that work of Jesus Christ.

It is a very serious thing partaking of the body of Jesus Christ and of the blood of Jesus Christ. We should really examine our hearts before we do so and always do it in a very reverent and worshipful manner.

(Smith, 1982-85)

Come, Let Us Reason Together

Even a year prior to reading Chuck Smith's discussion on this passage, I had come to the same conclusion. A close examination of the Scripture has to lead to the belief that the scourging of the Savior had the purpose of our healing---physically, spiritually, emotionally, and mentally. His was a complete work. It is verified by the passages in Matthew,

1 Peter, and in 1 Corinthians, and many other passages in the Scripture. Does this mean we will never get sick and will always be healed? Read James 5: 13-16 again! Remember, this is a very complex topic and worthy of much deeper discussion. God is sovereign, and God is good, always good.

There are many, many other commentators who have objected and explained 1 Corinthians 11: 29-32 away or kind of ignored it. I wrongly believed them for most of my life, until I made the commitment to research it myself. We cannot sidestep what is written in His Word. We do have the right to choose to believe or not to believe. Let's progress further. Paul is not finished!

Verses 31,32:

> "But if we judged ourselves rightly, we would not be judged. But when we are judged, we are disciplined by the Lord so that we will not be condemned with the world."

We must judge ourselves rightly. That is what the Lord is commanding us to do...to examine ourselves correctly.

"If we judge ourselves rightly [correctly], we would not be judged."

Judged by whom? If we judge ourselves **incorrectly** who is going to judge us? The answer is…**God!** "We are disciplined by the Lord". We are corrected by Him.

Why?

"So that we will not be condemned with the world."

Time and again throughout the Bible, God pleads with humanity to turn away from our rebellion. He takes no pleasure in judging, but He is a holy God. He desires us to turn to Him and find an abundant life through faith in Christ. Here! NOW! In this life! On this earth! Our sin problem that has separated us from Him has been PAID IN FULL through Christ. It is a FREE gift to all. It is for you! Only Believe!

The Communion service is FAR more important than the meaningless ritual and tradition often espoused today. It deals directly with who Jesus is and what He accomplished on the cross. As a believer in Christ, studying these passages should excite and thrill you concerning the fantastic work accomplished for us by Christ. After examining yourself and determining that you do not wish to follow Christ, then according to the Word of God, it is far better for you not to take Communion, even if you are encouraged in a service to participate. Others, even leaders may tell you it is OK, but the Lord says you are responsible to examine yourself. Remember, as you decide, that the Lord's Supper was instituted by the Lord Himself on the night He was betrayed. Paul received his instructions directly from the Lord. Yes, they seem harsh, depending on your viewpoint, and you have the right to believe whatever you like. No church authority, person or institution has authority over the direct Word of God from Christ Himself.

Again, in the United States, God has allowed us the freedom to read the Bible. Do NOT believe what I have written just on face value. Carefully search the Scriptures yourself, as I have. Pray and ask God to lead you into His truth. Look up the words in the original languages. Read commentaries, but check everything according to the Scripture. I have done all these things, and have come to my own conclusions. My personal conclusion after extensive study and prayer?

I BELIEVE HE SHED HIS BLOOD FOR MY SINS AND I KNOW HE HAS FORGIVEN ME AND DWELLS WITH ME AND IN ME!!!

I BELIEVE AND KNOW HIS SCOURGING WAS FOR MY HEALING: INSTANTLY, GRADUALLY, IN STAGES, AS I GROW IN GRACE; WHENEVER HE CHOOSES; HOWEVER HE CHOOSES!!!

I KNOW HE IS COMING AGAIN FOR THOSE WHO HAVE BELIEVED IN HIM AND ARE HIS TRUE DISCIPLES!

I BELIEVE!

THE NECESSITY OF FAITH

Every blessing of God to us is only accomplished by faith. It is the absolute essential ingredient necessary to have a relationship with God. Regarding this topic, I will let the Scripture speak for itself:

> Now faith is the assurance of things hoped for, the conviction of things not seen. For by it the men of old gained approval. By faith we understand that the worlds were prepared by the word of God, so that what is seen was not made out of things which are visible.
>
> Hebrews 11:1

> "And without faith it is IMPOSSIBLE to please Him, for he who comes to God must believe that He [God] is and that He is a rewarder of those who seek Him."
>
> Hebrews 11:6

> "Behold, as for the proud, his soul is not right within him; But the righteous will live by his faith."
>
> Habakkuk 2:4

"For whatever is born of God overcomes the world;
and this is the victory that overcomes the world...
our faith!"

1 John 5:4

In Mark 9:22, The boy's father said to Jesus

"'But if You can do anything, take pity on us and help us!' And
Jesus said to him, '"If You <u>CAN</u>?" <u>All things are possible
to him who BELIEVES'.</u>"

Do YOU believe? If so, then be it done unto you according to your faith, in Jesus' Name. Take the time you need to research the Scriptures and come to your own conclusions, as I have. Be willing to lay aside any pre-determined conclusions and ask God by His Spirit to reveal His truth to your heart.

PARTAKING OF COMMUNION AS A BELIEVER

As a follower of Christ, whether you are taking Communion in a church service, privately with your family, or in worship alone, embrace these teachings for an active, intimate celebration with your Lord. Set aside time to commune with Christ. Why are we in such a hurry? When our Lord and Savior is present in Spirit, is there really a rush?

1. Examine your heart before God.

2. In prayer, welcome Him to minister to you in any way He chooses.

3. Praise Him that He is with you and in you.

4. Meditate on His birth, life, death, burial, resurrection, and ascension. Often, He will bring specific Bible verses, worship songs, and hymns to your mind that will cause you to praise Him.

5. Understand that His scourging was for you and is an integral part of His sacrifice. His scourging was intentional and on purpose for your healing. Welcome and receive by faith any type of healing He brings, any way He chooses to bring it, any amount of time He chooses. Be open to a physical, mental, emotional, and spiritual touch. Ask Him by faith for specific areas you need. His body was broken for you. "By His stripes you are healed." Thank Him that He is your Healer.

(As you meditate on His body that was broken for you, break the bread and receive it with thanksgiving.)

6. Thank Him for paying the price for your sins, for dying on the cross. Tell Him you love Him, because His sacrifice was a result of God's passionate love for you. See Him on the cross dying for your sin that you might have freedom, forgiveness, and eternal life.

(In remembrance of Him, take the cup)

7. He is coming again and very soon. This time He is coming to receive you to Himself. Thank Him and praise Him.

8. Rest in His presence. Enjoy your communion with Him remembering His life, death, burial, resurrection, and ascension. Feast on favorite passages of the Bible related to His promise to come again for you. No need to rush.

"Those who wait for the Lord will gain new strength;
They will mount up with wings like eagles, they will run
and not get tired, they will walk and not become weary."
Isaiah 40: 31

Do you realize that you are communing with the Creator of the universe? He is intimately concerned about you and all your needs. Songs of praise may come to your mind. Sing them.

By way of opinion, according to James 5, I would personally have every Communion service in a church setting end with prayer for any person's spiritual, physical, or temporal needs, by faith giving God the opportunity to minister to the people He loves, which is everyone. Prayer should be offered even for those who are not followers of Christ if it is needed or requested. It is a very special time of intimacy with Christ and with other believers. Oh, that we could grasp the tremendous love of God for humanity, the love that caused Christ to go to the cross and provide a way back to peace with God.

Closing Comments

You can consult with many church leaders, theologians, and commentaries that will not agree with what is written here. I have carefully read most of the commentaries. My concern has been only one--what does the Bible say! As best as we could, we have kept personal opinion aside allowing the Scripture to speak for itself even in the original languages. Now the task is yours as to what to believe.

True Communion is an active, vibrant celebration with a risen Savior. You have walked with me through *The Body and the Blood,* and you are now able to take Communion whenever and wherever you choose, as often as you like, meeting all of the conditions, and enjoying all of the blessings that Christ secured for those who believe in Him. Rejoice, His riches and blessings abound for you.

God has…

"blessed you with EVERY spiritual blessing in the heavenlies in Christ Jesus."

Ephesians 1:3

PRAYER OF BLESSING FOR YOU

Eternal Father, Creator of heaven and earth, we come to you in the precious name of Jesus Christ, our Savior and Lord. We trust and pray that you will pour out your blessing on the readers of this book, drawing them closer to Jesus Christ, our Savior, Healer, and Coming King. Give them wisdom and insight as they study the Scripture passages and guide them in the truth, in only YOUR truth. We pray that Your Spirit will elevate each Communion service of the readers into a vibrant, active, intimate, exciting, reverent, holy celebration, and fellowship with the Savior of the world. We pray that receiving this teaching by faith will catapult each of us as individuals into new heights of Your wonderful presence, exalting Christ as our most glorious Savior. By faith help us to appropriate all of the blessings provided for us in His body and His blood, experiencing forgiveness and healing in all areas of our lives. We ask this in the wonderful name of Jesus Christ, our soon and coming King.

Amen and Amen!

COMMONLY ASKED QUESTIONS

Q: Should I allow my children to take Communion?

A: Children are covered under the Blood of Christ until the age of accountability; that age varies for each child. There is not one age for all children. You as the parent, raising your child in a godly manner, must make the determination as to whether you allow your children to take Communion, at what age and when they come to a personal faith in Jesus Christ. It is definitely a teaching opportunity, of which we hope and pray this book will help. Your church may have specific requirements regarding children which should be respected if you attend that church.

Q: Do I have to be a member of a specific church to take Communion?

A: Membership is required by some churches. The Bible is our final authority. You must be a member of the Body of Christ, having repented of your sins, received Jesus as Savior and Lord of your life. You are commanded to examine yourself in this regard. If you have chosen to attend a church that has specific conditions regarding Communion, you should respect those conditions as long as they are not in conflict with the Bible, which is the final authority.

Q: I have heard that the bread and the cup are symbolic only?

A: When our Lord instituted the Communion service, He held the bread in His hand. It was bread. He held the cup in His hand. It was wine. There is no suggestion from the Bible that they were anything more than symbols of His body and His blood; to go beyond is adding and modifying the Scripture, which we will not do. The beauty of the Communion celebration is that the Lord participates in it WITH us and IN us as we remember Him. The glory of the Communion service is His Presence. Nothing is more glorious than His presence. It is my opinion that we should be careful adding anything mystical to the elements. The presence of Christ is more than enough, and we should not distract from this. Others will disagree on this. Let each one be convinced in his own mind, but be careful not to add to the Scripture or the Communion practice anything that may diminish the Person of Christ.

Q: Does Communion have to be offered at a church and administered by a minister, a priest, or laity?

A: It is very special when the church takes Communion together in remembrance of our Lord. However, it also can be taken in your home with your family or alone. My wife and I often take Communion in our home, both together and alone, celebrating both His body for our protection and healing and His blood for the forgiveness of our sins, celebrating the entire person and work of Christ. Take and eat as often as you like. Remember, the bread and the cup have no special powers. The blessing of the Communion celebration is the PRESENCE of the Lord Himself. Whenever you take Communion, invite Him and give Him permission to do as He wills in every area of your life.

Q: Do the Bread and the Cup have to be unleavened bread and wine?

A: The bread and the cup are symbols of the body and blood of our Lord. Some congregations use a wafer, others a broken cracker. Usually, instead of wine, grape juice is used. Nothing in the Scripture suggests anything other than they are symbolic. Even in their symbolism, reverently remember the elements represent the body and the blood of Jesus Christ; do not take them carelessly. The beauty and awe of the Communion service is the Presence of Christ in the service with you as you remember and celebrate Him. Often with the bread, as I am meditating on the body of Christ that was scourged for my healing, when I break it, my spirit is flooded with praise and thanksgiving knowing He did paid this price for me.

Q: Should others deny me from taking Communion?

A: The study of this book gives you the conditions you need to know. You are responsible for examining yourself as Paul said. You are to judge yourself. I cannot and do not judge your heart for you. However, Paul states that you are to judge yourself <u>correctly</u>. It is not wise to publicly present yourself as someone you are not. If you judge yourself correctly, Paul says you will not be judged (by God). In other words, God is watching, desiring, and wanting you to judge yourself correctly. Notice in the 1 Corinthians passage how often it is repeated for you to examine and judge yourself. God wants YOU to be honest before Him. Some leaders, if they believe you are continuing in some sort of sin, may ask you not to take Communion. I would give special consideration to a minister, elders of your church, or a Christian friend you are working with if there is a concern. It would be good for you to respectfully listen to her or him. Leaders are responsible to give accurate, Biblical instruction to you and must examine their own lives as well.

A WORD TO THOSE WHO ADMINISTER COMMUNION

The Scripture is very clear that there are conditions for being worthy to take Communion. Each person is to examine himself/herself. The task and responsibility of you, the teacher, is to make sure that people know what the Scripture says. If you have **"divided the Word"** correctly and faithfully taught it, then the burden is on the person who takes Communion.

The Bible states that we who are teachers will incur a stricter judgment. As teachers, we are to be very careful that we are dividing the Word of God correctly. If we are not teaching Communion properly and therefore, those who take it do not understand the blessings and conditions of participating, then the responsibility is ours for not telling them. If, however, we have told them and taught them properly, then the responsibility of acting with knowledge and examining themselves correctly belongs to them.

Some of these teachings may very well be completely opposite from what you have been taught or believed. I came from a Conservative Mennonite background; you can probably guess that my journey was a long one. Once I accepted the Bible to be the absolute Word of God, then I felt an obligation to test everything I believed. If the Bible proved it, I kept it. If through diligent study, the Scripture could not support it, then I tossed it and replaced it with the truth. God, through Jesus Christ, by His precious Holy Spirit has brought me a long way. I know also that I have a very long way to go. I pray His blessings on you as you seek Him with all your heart and shepherd His beloved children.

References

Brown, M. (2005). Hebrew Rapha. *I am the Lord your healer.* Retrieved from https://www.AskDrBrown.org

Smith, C. (1972-75). *Sermon: I Corinthians 11:25.* [Audio file] Retrieved from https://www.blueletterbible.org/Comm/smith_ chuck/c2000 1Cr//1Cr011.cfm

Smith, C. (1982-85). *Sermon: Matthew 27.* [Audio file] Retrieved from https://www.blueletterbible.org/Comm/Smith_chuck/ c2000_Mat/Mat

Strobel, L. (1998). Introduction. *The case for Christ* (pp. 9-15). Grand Rapids, MI: Thomas Nelson.

Strong, J. (2001a). The new Strong's expanded dictionary of the words in the Greek New Testament. *The new Strong's expanded exhaustive concordance of the Bible* (pp. 22 -732). Nashville, TN: Thomas Nelson.

Strong, J. (2001b). The new Strong's expanded dictionary of the words in the Hebrew Bible. *The new Strong's expanded exhaustive concordance of the Bible* (pp. 79-265). Nashville, TN: Thomas Nelson.

ABOUT THE AUTHOR

Randy J. Widrick resides in Upstate NY with his wife of 39 years, Josephine. They have been actively involved in teaching, preaching, writing, and music ministry in churches in Upstate NY, Colorado, and Arizona since 1980 and currently are members of Hands of Hope Ministries, Free Methodist Church.

Made in the USA
Middletown, DE
15 April 2019